COLLECTOR'S EDITION

SATURDAY NIGHT LIVE

45 YEARS

CELEBRATING *SATURDAY NIGHT LIVE*

The first broadcast of a new comedy show from NBC's studios in New York City happened almost two years after the launch of a new magazine about the fascinating people who make movies, musical recordings and TV to entertain us: *People*. Over 45 seasons of its run as the most successful comedy show on late-night TV, *SNL* and its stars—from John Belushi and Gilda Radner to Tina Fey and Kate McKinnon—have appeared countless times in the pages of this magazine, and we are proud today to present a special edition dedicated to the best comedy sketches from every decade of *SNL*, the most popular celebrity hosts, the memorable (and most danceable) dance-musical performances and the unforgettable characters whose funny phrases have entered the national lexicon. Now isn't *that* special! We also spoke to veteran comedy writer and *SNL* alum Alan Zweibel, who shared a first-person view of the creation of some of those characters during the show's first seasons. Happy anniversary, *SNL*, we're looking forward to many more seasons of laughter.

CONTENTS

SATURDAY NIGHT LIVE

Regularly Scheduled Laughter

MORE THAN JUST ENTERTAINING, *SATURDAY NIGHT LIVE* HAS BEEN A RELIABLE COMFORT DURING TROUBLED TIMES AND A HUMOROUS AGENT FOR CHANGE—NOW MORE THAN EVER **BY LISA RUSSELL**

W"WE DON'T GO ON because we're ready," producer Lorne Michaels famously said about *Saturday Night Live*. "We go on because it's 11:30." But in fact, since its Oct. 11, 1975, debut the late-night comedy show and its Not Ready for Prime Time Players have indeed been ready. Ready for anything: to take on

the status quo, to make light of uncomfortable truths, to cut to the quick and make fast, funny sense of the week that just was. To seamlessly pivot and do the show from home during the COVID-19 pandemic. And always, to entertain. When controversial comedian George Carlin walked out to deliver the first monologue, audiences were put on notice. This was entirely new TV, giving voice to a generation of comics and writers who were itching to get their hands on mainstream media and shake it up. *SNL* was their answer to decades of polished, professional, don't-rock-the-boat talk shows and variety hours with well-known hosts like Lawrence Welk, Ed Sullivan, Carol Burnett and Johnny Carson. "We were an Off-Broadway variety show, and we were saying what we wanted to say about Nixon and Three Mile Island [the nuclear accident then in the news] and Ford and then Carter," recalls former *SNL* writer Alan Zweibel, who was there for the show's first five seasons. But mostly, he says, "we were putting on the best possible show we could."

LONG REACH
On the March 7, 2020, show—the last *SNL* of the season performed before a live audience—host Daniel Craig and Kate McKinnon were soap opera actors socially distancing themselves while playing lovers.

BAD TIMES AND GOOD Above: In addition to the indignities of a year that had already seen political unrest and a global epidemic, "Weekend Update" host Michael Che bemoaned the plague of "murder hornets" that scientists predicted were headed our way. That was on one of *SNL's* at-home episodes, which were taped remotely at the cast's homes after the show's N.Y.C. studio was closed because of COVID-19. Below: Musical guest Miley Cyrus performed a cover of Pink Floyd's "Wish You Were Here" during a time of widespread social lockdowns.

Thus, Chevy Chase took pratfall after pratfall as clumsy President Gerald Ford (who was an athlete in real life), while John Belushi brought his manic energy to the Samurai Futaba or Bill Murray showed up to sing the made-up lyrics to the *Star Wars* theme. Or maybe Dan Aykroyd and Jane Curtin's Coneheads dropped by, aliens from the planet Remulak trying desperately to make sense of life in modern-day America.

SNL's mix of topicality and satire has served as a mirth-making social barometer from the beginning. Chase's Ford paved the way for Aykroyd's parody of humble Jimmy Carter, Dana Carvey's puckish George H.W. Bush, Phil Hartman and Darrell Hammond's lecherous Bill Clinton, Will Ferrell's dithering George W. Bush, Fred Armisen and Jay Pharoah's conflicted Barack Obama and, recently, Alec Baldwin's triumphant run as a bombastic Donald Trump. And those are just the Presidents. Who can forget Kate McKinnon's tortured Hillary Clinton or Tina Fey's incomparable, lookalike take on Alaska governor Sarah Palin?

The list of beloved characters has evolved too, of course—Eddie Murphy's Gumby, Molly Shannon's schoolgirl Mary Katherine Gallagher, Tim Meadows's Ladies Man and Kristen Wiig's Target Lady, to name just a few. Through seasons

THE DOCTOR IS IN
Brad Pitt won an Emmy nomination for portraying COVID-19 expert Dr. Anthony Fauci on *SNL*. During the April 2020 spoof, he thanked "all the older women in America who have sent me supportive, inspiring and sometimes graphic emails." Pitt then took off his wig and thanked the real Dr. Fauci for his "calm and...clarity in this unnerving time."

hailed as triumphs and those derided as Saturday Night Dead, "if you look at any era, you'll find people who are not only hilarious but hilarious in different ways than people before them or since are," Zweibel says. "There's a uniqueness that they all bring."

And a sense of daring. *SNL* has often been in front of the curve of public opinion. When Terry Sweeney joined the cast for the 1985-86 season, bringing his uncanny impersonation of then First Lady Nancy Reagan, he became the first openly gay man on network TV. "No one else in entertainment was saying it," Sweeney told *People* at the time. "I was tired of invisibility." The pendulum had swung so far on the LGBTQ movement that by 2012 when Kate McKinnon joined the cast, the fact that she was openly gay caused nary a stir—but her hilarious impersonation of Supreme Court Justice Ruth Bader Ginsburg did. More recently the 2019 promotion of Bowen Yang from writer to player was notable less for the fact that he's also gay than for his status as the show's first member of another underrepresented group—actors of Chinese-American descent.

At other times *SNL* has needed a little prodding. Though it has had black male cast members from the start—Garrett ("baseball's been berry berry good to me") Morris was a member of the founding

crew—in 2013 African-American cast members Kenan Thompson and Jay Pharoah went public, asking why there hadn't been a female black cast member since Maya Rudolph departed in 2007. Especially when someone was needed to play First Lady Michelle Obama and superstar Beyoncé. Under pressure, Michaels held secret auditions and hired Sasheer Zamata and writers LaKendra Tookes and Leslie Jones. (Jones became a cast member in the fall of 2014.)

Other controversies have seemed almost appropriately comical in comparison. Two cast members—Charles Rocket in 1981 and Jenny Slate in 2009—were fired after dropping the "F-bomb" on air. (Censors do, in fact, stay up late for *SNL.*) Rocker Elvis Costello was reportedly "banned for life" after performing a song critical of media. (He eventually came back.) A 1988 sketch written by Conan O'Brien and starring host Matthew Broderick and most of the male cast members set a TV record by using the word "penis" 43 times. In 2004 pop princess Ashlee Simpson got caught—gasp!—lip syncing. On a more serious note, in 1990 Nora

'LOOK AT ME. I STARTED AS THE SON OF A SIMPLE WEALTHY SLUMLORD AND GREW TO BECOME A BILLIONAIRE, A PRESIDENT AND THE WORLD'S LEADING EXPERT ON INFECTIOUS DISEASES'

—ALEC BALDWIN, ON *SNL* AS DONALD TRUMP

YOU HAVE TO LAUGH
Left: Political satire, like Alec Baldwin doing Donald Trump in October 2016, was part of what made *SNL* relevant 45 years ago and has continued to this day, no matter which party is in power.

Dunn refused to go on, in protest of what she called host Andrew Dice Clay's misogyny. She was joined by musical guest Sinéad O'Connor, who returned to *SNL* two years later and ripped up a picture of the Pope on live TV, earning headlines around the world and the outspoken enmity of Frank Sinatra.

Then, in March 2020, the lights went out in Studio 8H. In the wake of COVID-19, writers, cast members and producers retreated to their own homes, but they carried on for the remainder of their 45th season. Wiig hosted the Mother's Day finale show from her house in L.A., starting out with a bang in black sequins. Beck Bennett hosted the dating show "How Low Will You Go?" for those desperately horny under quarantine, and McKinnon's high school principal reluctantly served up Donald Trump's "valedictator" address to her graduating seniors. "I thought it was going to suck," admitted cast member Pete Davidson of *SNL's* WFH editions. But it did not suck.

Through the decades there has always been "Weekend Update" to look forward to. Since Chevy Chase first introduced *SNL's* news bulletin with "I'm Chevy Chase and you're not," the WU host chair has been the most prestigious position in the house. Hosted over the years by Curtin, Dennis Miller, Kevin Nealon, Jimmy Fallon, Poehler, Fey, Cecily Strong and SethMeyers, among others, it's where the show takes off the gloves and deploys its acid wit to say things that need to be said, after the polite company has gone to bed. It is where Leslie Jones, while calling attention to her sturdy physical stature, could outrageously declare, in 2014, that "back in the slave days, my love life would have been way better." It is where Fey popped up with comforting pandemic advice: "If you're baking cookies and you don't have any flour, you can just go to bed." For the past six years it is where white Colin Jost and Black Michael Che, *SNL's* co-head writers, have shared the desk, Jost playing a buttoned-up foil to Che's sly but penetrating take on systemic racism and other injustices. "So let me get this straight," Che recently wondered aloud. "I gotta try to survive this summer, the coronavirus, the police, basic cardio and now big-ass murder hornets. Why do I feel like I'm living in the Old Testament?"

SNL, as necessary as ever.

'WE'RE FROM FRANCE'
—THE CONEHEADS

THE CONEHEADS
Originally from the planet Remulak, parental units Beldar (Dan Aykroyd) and Prymaat (Jane Curtin) and daughter Connie (Laraine Newman) spent much of their energy consuming "mass quantities" of food (here, with Bill Murray as game show host Richard Dawson).

THE WORLD WAS CHANGING. In 1974, when Johnny Carson, then the king of late-night TV, decided that he no longer wanted reruns of *The Tonight Show* to air on weekend nights, NBC executives scrambled to fill Saturday's graveyard hours, from 11:30 p.m. to 1 a.m. They had little to lose: No one was watching TV at that hour, so the brass handed the broadcast keys to a bunch of funny misfits from the underground comedy scene that had sprung up around *National Lampoon* magazine and comedy troupes Second City in Chicago and the Groundlings in L.A. Created by Canadian comedy writer Lorne Michaels, *NBC's Saturday Night* (as it was then called) premiered without fanfare on Oct. 11, 1975, but it almost immediately connected with American youth disillusioned by Vietnam and Watergate and launched a new generation of comedy stars.

It was the first show written and performed for people who had grown up watching television and were ready for a radical reinvention. At a time when TV was called "the boob tube," featuring tepid hits like *The Six Million Dollar Man* and *The Bionic Woman, SNL* turned the medium's tired tropes on their heads. The result was explosive. "In my heart of hearts I truly believe that the people at NBC do not know what they have there," Michaels said in 1979. "No more than RCA knew what they had when they had Elvis Presley."

Not that those creating this electrifying improvisational comedy had a much clearer idea of the new guerrilla theater they were birthing. Sure, absurdist situational sketches like "The Coneheads," featuring a clan of aliens with typical Earth-family problems like truculent teenagers, were a no (make that very large) brainer. But no one in the famously fraught, pharmaceutical-friendly offices above the network's Studio 8H at 30 Rockefeller Center really knew what the reaction would be to letting Chevy Chase, the show's first breakout star, impersonate the sitting President, Gerald R. Ford, as a bumbling, good-natured idiot. (Positive, it turned

'CHEEBURGER, CHEEBURGER!'
Above: Customers (from left, Garret Morris, Curtin and Gilda Radner) had just three options when ordering from Greek owner Pete (Belushi) at the Olympia Cafe: "Cheeburgers," "No Coke, Pepsi!" and "No fries, cheeps!"

SAMURAI FUTABA
Right: Though Belushi's easily excitable warrior spoke only (mock) Japanese, in more than 15 skits his wildly inventive (and sometimes scary) swordplay saved the day when the samurai moonlighted in such nontraditional jobs as tailor, stockbroker and (with Dan Aykroyd) hit man.

LAND SHARK
Above: Plumber, candygram—as the Land Shark, Chevy Chase used tame, lame excuses to lure single women into opening their doors to a gruesome death.

NICK WINTERS, THE LOUNGE SINGER
Above right: Bill Murray was at his unctuous best as a small-time, small-talent singer who put words to the *Star Wars* theme. At the piano (rear), *SNL* band member Paul Schaffer.

BEHIND THE SCENES: FREE TICKETS

In November 1978 *SNL* fans stood in long lines for hours to win a treasured ticket into Studio 8H. Despite a lottery, lines for standby tickets remained.

'I DO REMEMBER WHEN I FIRST SAW THE SHOW. IT CAME ON, AND I THOUGHT, "THEY'VE DONE IT!" THEY DID THE ZEITGEIST; THEY DID WHAT WAS OUT THERE... THIS KIND OF NEW COMEDY'
—STEVE MARTIN

out. With an eye on the gargantuan ratings, Ford's press secretary Ron Nessen was the first political figure to host the show, and his boss even delivered a taped "Live from New York, it's *Saturday Night*!" intro. Was it mean for Gilda Radner to make fun of newswoman Barbara Walters's speech impediment as Baba Wawa? How about the deliberately fractured, undoubtedly offensive gibberish that John Belushi passed off as Japanese in his famed "Samurai" skits? Mainstream young American viewers didn't seem bothered; in fact, they were highly amused.

Saturday Night Live (renamed in 1977) played by its own rules, and the audience understood and loved its cast of comedians for it. From the very first broadcast, hosted by the counterculture comedian George Carlin, the show aimed for rock and roll anarchy—and, ironically, quickly made the renegade band of Not Ready for Prime Time Players into mainstream stars. Belushi was soon on the big screen in *Animal House*, and, with fellow cast member Dan Aykroyd, in *The Blues Brothers*. Radner had her own Broadway show. Curtin has been on television virtually ever since. And is there anywhere Bill Murray hasn't been? Even the show's deliberately cheesy offscreen announcer Don Pardo became something of a household name.

"We wanted to redefine comedy the way the Beatles redefined what being a pop star was," Michaels said. "That required not pandering, and it also required removing neediness, the need to please. It was like, we're only going to please those people who are like us. The presumption was there were a lot of people like us. And that turned out to be so."

STEVE MARTIN
>SNL<
THE '70s
SUPERHOST

BREAKOUT PERFORMER
In frequent *SNL* appearances, comedian Steve Martin walked like funky Egyptian King Tut (above); with Aykroyd, tried to seduce American "foxes" (here, Radner, Newman and Curtin) as Czechoslovakian brothers Georg and Yortuk Festrunk (right); and touted therapeutic bloodletting on "Theodoric of York, Medieval Barber (below)."

'WE'RE TWO WILD AND CRAZY GUYS'
—THE FESTRUNK BROTHERS

'I'D LIKE TO WRITE A LETTER TO THE PEOPLE OUT THERE AS IF I WAS WRITING HOME FROM CAMP. I'D WANT THEM TO KNOW I WAS HAVING A GOOD TIME'
—GILDA RADNER, 1977

'IT'S ALWAYS SOMETHING'
Weekend Update consumer-affairs correspondent Roseanne Roseannadanna's beat? Going off topic to discuss hygiene, bodily functions and the time she found a toenail in her hamburger.

BEHIND THE SCENES: ON-SET
As host in 1977, Minnesota Vikings quarterback Fran Tarkenton discussed strategy with Newman, Curtin and Radner.

1946-1989

GILDA RADNER

THE *SNL* TRAILBLAZER COMBINED SWEETNESS WITH COMIC SAUCINESS

She was the first female *SNL* cast member to become America's favorite. But unlike others to follow, like the cerebral, satiric Tina Fey or the sly, impenetrable Kristen Wiig, Radner's strength lay in her inherent goofiness and the lingering effects of growing up chubby, she once explained. Whether she was mugging as a high school wallflower or letting it rip as punk rocker Candy Slice (a character based on Patti Smith), there was no disguising Radner's lack of guile. "The same vulnerability that hurts her is what will make her a star," said the show's creator Lorne Michaels. Radner spent only five years on *SNL*, for which she won an Emmy in 1978, before going on to her own Broadway show, *Gilda Radner—Live from New York*. While filming the 1982 comedy *Hanky Panky*, she met actor Gene Wilder, and she wed him in 1984. "My life went from black-and-white to Technicolor," said Radner, who made three movies with Wilder. But the love she had finally found was tragically short-lived. Radner died of ovarian cancer, at just 42, in 1989.

NEWSWORTHY
She came to appreciate Radner's "Baba Wawa" impersonation, but at first newswoman Barbara Walters "wasn't so thrilled."

EMILY'S LIST
The topics misheard by Radner's hearing-impaired Emily Litella included "youth in Asia" (euthanasia) and "presidential erections" (elections). Never mind.

THE DEVIL MADE HER DO IT
Above: Newman made heads spin as the child possessed by Satan who incited a pair of priests (actor Thalmus Rasulala, center, and guest Richard Pryor) to violence in a 1975 *Exorcist* parody.

‘SAVE THE LIVER’
Top left: Aykroyd memorably played the revered French chef Julia Child in a 1978 skit in which the TV star sliced her hand and bled to death on the kitchen counter.

POINT TAKEN
Left: “Weekend Update” hosts Curtin and Aykroyd appeared in the debate segment “Point Counterpoint” (borrowed from *60 Minutes*). She’d deliver an impassioned, reasonable argument about current events. His rejoinder: “Jane, you ignorant slut.”

‘OH, NOOOOOO!’
Right: Things often ended very badly for gullible clay figure Mr. Bill (far right, with dog Spot), often at the hands of Sluggo (left).

1949-1982

JOHN BELUSHI

AN APPETITE FOR DESTRUCTION TOOK AN EXPLOSIVE TALENT EARLY

"If people want to think that I'm a drug-crazed anarchist, and it brings them into the theaters, that's fine," John Belushi said in 1980. "Actually I'm a pretty boring guy most of the time." Boring? No one who laid eyes on his subversive comedy on *SNL* would call him anything other than game-changing. Born in Chicago, the veteran of the Second City comedy troupe brought to *SNL* a mini cast of unforgettable characters, often playing comic foil to his good friend Dan Aykroyd, with whom he created the Blues Brothers sketch that went on to become the 1980 film and box office hit. Unapologetically reveling in his appetites—for food, booze, the blues—Belushi was both loved and fretted over by those who knew him well. The ending, when it came in 1982, was textbook tawdry. Belushi was found in a bungalow at L.A.'s Chateau Marmont dead of an overdose of cocaine and heroin at 33. "It was very sad," said Jane Curtin. But unlike his outsize talent, "it wasn't shocking."

SOUL MEN
Aykroyd and Belushi debuted the Blues Brothers in 1978.

THE GODFATHER
Playing Marlon Brando's gravel-voiced Don Corleone, Belushi (with Murray) could hardly be heard.

TURN IN YOUR PHASERS
The 1976 *Star Trek* parody, costarring Elliott Gould, earned Belushi props for his devastating portrayal of William Shatner learning that *Star Trek* was being canceled.

BEHIND THE SCENES: WARDROBE

"He felt [the Killer Bee costume] was so humiliating, and it really came through in the character," said an *SNL* staffer.

'I HIRED HIM BECAUSE HE WALKED INTO MY OFFICE... AND SAID, "I CAN'T STAND TELEVISION," AND THAT WAS JUST THE KIND OF ABUSE I WANTED TO HEAR'

—LORNE MICHAELS

'WE WERE JUST PUTTING ON THE MUSIC WE WERE LISTENING TO. WE WERE FANS'
—LORNE MICHAELS

IT'S ONLY ROCK AND ROLL
Left: On the second episode of *SNL,* host Paul Simon (right) brought former partner Art Garfunkel out to duet on three of their old hits, including "The Boxer." Above: In December 1977 British rebel Elvis Costello (with the Attractions) got himself banned from the show for performing his anti-mainstream-media rant "Radio Radio" instead of the agreed-on "Less Than Zero." Producer Michaels finally let him back in Studio 8H in 1989. Below: Ray Charles was a host and musical guest in 1975, performing a melody including "Oh, What a Beautiful Mornin'." Right: Proto-punk/poet Patti Smith was six months into becoming a cult figure with her 1975 debut album, *Horses,* when she delivered riveting versions of Van Morrison's "Gloria" and the Who's "My Generation."

DREAM JOB
"I have a movie coming out that took three years, okay?" says Zweibel (on the *SNL* set in 1979 with Laraine Newman, John Belushi and others). "A book, if you're lucky, takes two years. But to write something on Saturday and it's on the air half an hour later, it brings out a certain amount of adrenaline." Left: with one of two Emmys he won for *SNL* in the 1970s.

FIRST PERSON

VETERAN COMEDY WRITER AND *SNL* ALUM ALAN ZWEIBEL—AUTHOR OF THE NEW MEMOIR *LAUGH LINES: MY LIFE HELPING FUNNY PEOPLE BE FUNNIER*—TALKED TO *PEOPLE* ABOUT BEING IN ON THE GROUND FLOOR FOR THE CREATION OF A TV CLASSIC **BY LISA RUSSELL**

When *Saturday Night Live* first launched in 1975, did the cast members already have characters they could play?

Alan Zweibel: It was a combination. John Belushi came to the show with the samurai character, for instance. I believe it was the seventh show we ever did, and Richard Pryor was the host, when Belushi did the first sketch, "Samurai Hotel." And it was very successful. A few shows later Buck Henry was coming to town to host. I had worked in a delicatessen while I was writing for comedians up in the Catskills, to supplement the great living I was making, selling jokes for $7 apiece. Lorne Michaels said, "Do you think you could write 'Samurai Delicatessen?'" I said sure, and then I wrote all the other ones—"Samurai Night Fever," "Samurai Tailor," all of that.

How did you come up with other famous characters?

Gilda Radner and I created Roseanne Roseannadanna together. If you remember, on "Weekend Update" Roseannadanna got a letter every week from a guy named Richard Feder in Fort Lee, N.J.—that's the name of my real brother-in-law. For Emily Litella [Radner's perennially confused senior citizen], she was

impersonating a nanny she had when she was growing up. Her nickname was Dibby. Gilda would put me on the phone with Dibby, and it was like speaking to Emily Litella. She would get things wrong. She didn't hear things exactly right. Gilda was a great writer. She would take a red pencil, like a schoolmarm, and edit my scripts. She would take it to a different level.

Did you know you were part of something great?
Lorne gives you all the liberties in the world, for casting your sketches and music and wardrobe. I've been fortunate to have been a part of a lot of things that have been successful, but walking into that building, the very first day of *SNL* in 1975 was still the most exciting thing in the world.

THIS INTERVIEW HAS BEEN EDITED AND CONDENSED.

"'LET'S JUST MAKE EACH OTHER LAUGH. AND IF WE DO, WE'LL PUT IT ON TELEVISION." THOSE WERE THE FIRST WORDS I REMEMBER LORNE MICHAELS SAYING'
—ALAN ZWEIBEL

'SCHWING!'
Together, Mike Myers (left) and Dana Carvey achieved great *SNL* fame as basement metal heads and talk show hosts Wayne Campbell and Garth Algar of *Wayne's World*.

Saturday Night Live
The Best of the '80s

MONKEY BUSINESS
On "Sprockets," Myers's jaded German talk show host invariably asked guests like Ben Stiller (as Eddie Munster) to "touch my monkey."

THINGS WERE ABOUT TO GET MESSY. As the '70s drew to a close, *SNL* producer Lorne Michaels informed the brass at NBC that he was simply exhausted and needed some time off. He figured a year would do it and that the show could take a hiatus with him. The head office had other ideas. Brandon Tartikoff, head of NBC Entertainment, informed Michaels that *SNL* would go on without him, and—surprise!—associate producer Jean Doumanian would be taking over as his replacement. Michaels was upset, to say the least—and so was the star cast he had so painstakingly assembled. They all quit, along with most of the writers.

That left Doumanian, who had been with the show for five years, mostly as a talent booker, with a clean slate to begin the sixth season. She hired mostly lackluster new performers—do you remember Denny Dillon, Gail Matthius and Patrick Weathers?—while passing on the likes of Jim Carrey and John Goodman. (Carrey has since hosted three times, Goodman an astounding 13.) Doumanian did, however, give the okay to one very, very good hire. A young, brash comedian from Long Island "starting calling me," recalled talent coordinator Neil Levy. "I told him, 'I'm sorry, we're not auditioning anymore.' But he called again the next day, and he would go into this whole thing about how he had 18 brothers and sisters and how they were counting on him to get this job. And he would call every day for a week. And I finally decided I would use him as an extra." On Dec. 13, 1980, Eddie Murphy made his debut on *SNL*.

Despite Murphy's obvious brilliance—he was promoted to a repertory player just six weeks after that cameo—Doumanian's reign lasted only 12 episodes, most of them forgettable. "The shows were just not watchable," said

'ISN'T THAT SPECIAL?'
—ENID STRICT, THE CHURCH LADY

SUNDAY SCHOOL
Carvey carved out his own niche as the purse-lipped puritanical Church Lady.

'[MY] VERY FIRST NIGHT WAS A CRISIS. THE "CHURCH LADY" WAS GOING TO BE THE LAST SKETCH ON IN THE DRESS REHEARSAL... IN OTHER WORDS, THE DUMPING GROUND. BUT THEN IT KILLED IN DRESS, AND THEY MOVED IT UP TO BE THE VERY FIRST SKETCH'
—**DANA CARVEY**

NBC president Fred Silverman. Enter Dick Ebersol, part of the team that had originally created *SNL*. He fired the entire cast except for Murphy and Joe Piscopo, and relied on Murphy's indelible characters—Gumby, Mr. Robinson and Buckwheat—and Piscopo's loving homage to Frank Sinatra to carry the show. "I can never quite describe the thrill of working with Eddie Murphy live on the set of *SNL*," Piscopo said later. "We were like two college roommates cramming for a final—we both got punchy and started riffing, and some of the best stuff came out of that." They bowed out together as well, with Murphy departing mid-season and Piscopo leaving the show at the end of the ninth season. Luckily by that time Ebersol had managed to bring in names like Billy Crystal, Martin Short and Christopher Guest. When he left in 1985 (Ebersol would head up NBC Sports and produce the Olympics), *SNL* had regained its footing.

That year Michaels returned, adding even more talent—Phil Hartman, Dana Carvey, Nora Dunn and, in 1989, Mike Myers. "I remember very clearly when Mike Myers showed up," *SNL* writer Conan O'Brien recalled in Tom Shales's 2002 book *Live from New York*. "[He] described this character he had named Wayne who had a cable show in his basement and the show was called *Wayne's World*. ... I thought, 'This poor kid is going to have to learn the hard way.'" As if. It was soon easy to see: *SNL* was back on track, as funny and fearless as ever.

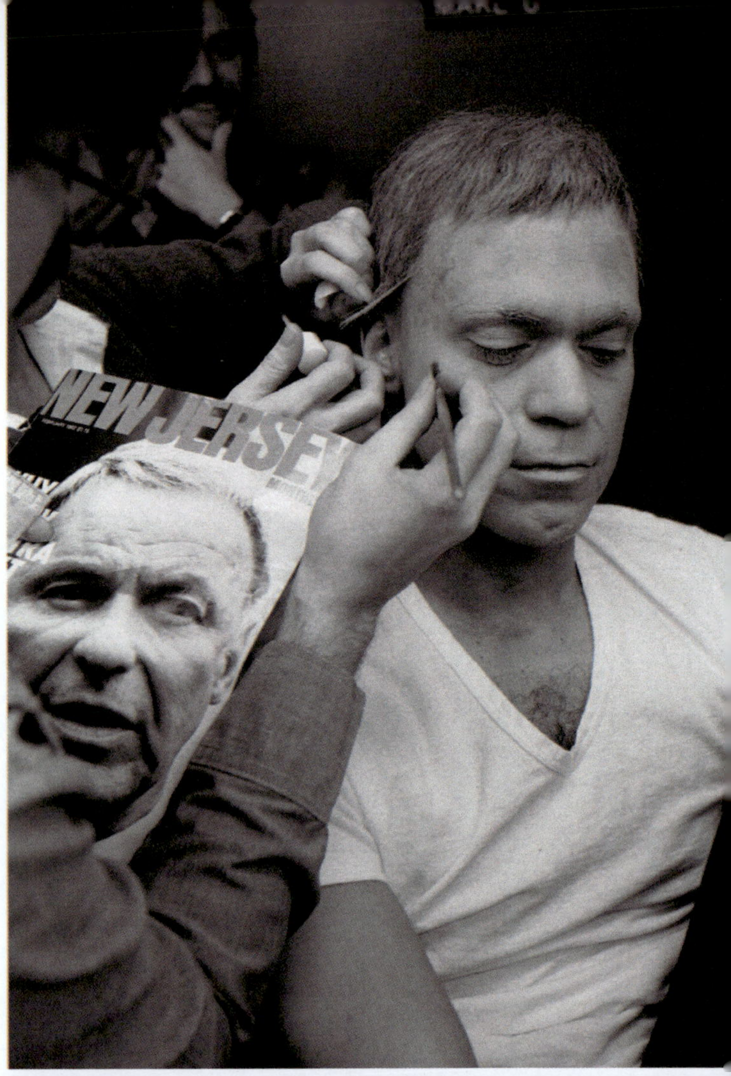

BEHIND THE SCENES: THE CREW

Above left: Makeup artists transformed Joe Piscopo to do his signature impersonation of Frank Sinatra in 1983. Above: In "Pumping Up with Hans & Franz," Austrian bodybuilding instructors Hans (Carvey, left) and Franz (Kevin Nealon, kneeling) welcomed customer Victoria Jackson with help from stagehands.

THE SWEENEY SISTERS
Left: During the 1988 Christmas show, lounge-singing siblings Candy (Jan Hooks, left) and Liz Sweeney (Nora Dunn, right) ended up in jail with a streetwalker (a bewigged Melanie Griffith).

'STOP! OH, NO MORE! THESE WORDS ENTER MY EARS LIKE DAGGERS! YOU'VE RIPPED APART MY SOUL LIKE A RABID DACHSHUND RIPPING INTO A BABY PIGLET!'
—THE MASTER THESPIAN

HOME ALONE
Above: His father was President when host Ron Reagan Jr. stripped to his skivvies for a 1986 spoof of Tom Cruise in *Risky Business.*

FOR ART'S SAKE
Left: What excuse did idiotic, egomaniacal "Shakespearean" actor Master Thespian (Jon Lovitz) give for duping lovers and double-dealing his enemies? "Acting!"

ALL WRONG
As Tommy Flanagan, head of Pathological Liars Anonymous, Lovitz defended Filipino dictator Ferdinand Marcos to "Weekend Update" host Dennis Miller.

'SHE WAS FUNNY, BEAUTIFUL AND STAGGERINGLY TALENTED'
—KEVIN NEALON

EVERYWOMAN
"We always thought of her as the female Phil Hartman [with whom Hooks often appeared]—she could play anything and do anything," said castmate Jon Lovitz.

1957-2014
JAN HOOKS

THE SOUTHERNER REMAINS A GUIDING LIGHT TO THOSE WHO CAME LATER

The Georgia-bred actress trained with L.A.'s Groundlings before joining *SNL* in 1986. Soon she was one half (with Nora Dunn) of the singing Sweeney Sisters, lovably garrulous losers plying their repertoire at hotel lounges across America. After five years of spot-on impressions of Sinéad O'Connor, Tammy Faye Bakker and Kathie Lee Gifford, among dozens, Hooks left to appear on *Designing Women* and had a recurring role on *3rd Rock from the Sun* (starring another alum, Jane Curtin). Her shining talent should have paved the way to a much brighter future, said Tina Fey, who sought Hooks out in 2010 to play Jenna Maroney's mother on *30 Rock*. "It made me mad at the time how available she was," Fey recalled. Like the show's male veterans, "Jan deserved a big movie career." When former cast member Kristen Wiig, who went on to the blockbuster *Bridesmaids,* hosted *SNL* in 2014—three days after Hooks's death from throat cancer at age 57—she introduced a video tribute to the comedian: "She was one of the best that ever was, and her influence is clear in every one of us who has been here since," said Wiig.

SPOT-ON
Apropos of nothing, "Nobody could make a waffle like Bert Lahr," Hooks's Bette Davis once said.

UNGODLY
Hooks was a weepy Tammy Faye Bakker with preacher husband Jim (Phil Hartman) in 1987.

IRREVERENT
A highlight of Hooks as Kathie Lee Gifford (here, with Dana Carvey as Regis Philbin) was the actress singing "I Didn't Evolve from You" to a monkey.

MORE COWLICK
Above: Martin Short's hyperactive nerd Ed Grimley, don'tcha know, was as inexplicably addicted to playing the triangle as he was to *Wheel of Fortune* host Pat Sajak.

NINE LIVES
From 1989 to 1993, Toonces the Cat Who Could Drive did just that—usually off a cliff.

'YOU LOOK MAHVELOUS'
—BILLY CRYSTAL AS FERNANDO LAMAS

SMOOTH OPERATOR
Billy Crystal (left), as Argentinian actor Fernando Lamas, entertained guests (like cohosts Mr. T, center, and wrestler Hulk Hogan) at his Fernando's Hideaway nightclub.

'[IN THE NBC MEN'S ROOM] YOU COULD SEE IN PENCIL ON THE WALL, "EDDIE MURPHY NO. 1"... I NEVER MET ANYBODY SO SURE THAT ONCE HE GOT HIS FOOT IN THE DOOR HE WAS GOING ALL THE WAY'

—NEIL LEVY, TALENT COORDINATOR

IN THE HOOD
Opposite: The yellow sweater was familiar, but that was about it. Eddie Murphy's "Mr. Robinson's Neighborhood" was a riotous take on the milquetoast *Mister Rogers' Neighborhood.*

EASY BEING GREEN
Left: In the '60s, he'd been a sweet TV claymation figure beloved by kids. Murphy's version was a bitter, cigar-chomping, foul-mouthed has-been who had to constantly remind people: He was Gumby, damn it!

FAN FAVORITES
Below left: Murphy's Little Richard Simmons (rock and roller Little Richard meets aerobics star Richard Simmons) and James Brown (below right), host of "James Brown's Celebrity Hot Tub Party," were delightfully absurd.

THE BEST MUSICAL PERFORMANCES
SNL
THE '80s

SOMETHING FOR EVERYONE

Clockwise from left: Avant-garde composer Philip Glass went mainstream for a 1986 performance of "Lightning." Rolling Stones guitarist Keith Richards thrashed his way through tracks from his first solo record, 1988's *Talk Is Cheap.* Queen's 1982 visit marked the band's final live performance in America with singer Freddie Mercury. In 1984 prank-rockers Spinal Tap delivered "Christmas with the Devil" and "Big Bottom." Asked about the former song, bassist Harry Shearer joked, "A man's relationship with the devil is a very private affair. It's not something you wear about on your sleeve."

VOX
VOX
VOX

ST. MONIC
AUTUMN FE
DANCE
SATURDAY NIGHT LIVE
The BEST of the '90s

SHE'S GOT THIS
She was awkward, she was oblivious, but as Catholic schoolgirl Mary Katherine Gallagher, Molly Shannon (with Chris Farley) was indeed, as she declared, a "superstar."

A AS THE '80S ENDED, STALWARTS Jan Hooks, Dana Carvey, Kevin Nealon and Phil Hartman were still delivering impeccable impressions—Carvey's spot-on George H.W. Bush and Hartman's pitch-perfect Clinton—while Nealon offered a sly, straight-man take on "Weekend Update." And Mike Myers's endearing, enduring "Wayne's World," costarring Carvey, would produce two hit movies. But as the new decade began, the show's ratings were the worst they'd been in years.

To shake things up, producer Lorne Michaels brought in a posse of young guns, the twentysomething bad boys of "bro" humor—Adam Sandler, David Spade, Chris Rock, Chris Farley and Rob Schneider—creating the largest cast that had ever filled the stage. Sandler donned a black cape to play Opera Man, singing booming commentary on news stories in an ersatz Italian accent. Spade winged insults at celebrities in "Hollywood Minute." Rock hosted a public-access cable show called "I'm Chillin'" with Farley, who generally threw himself around with surprising physicality for a man of his girth. Schneider was Richard, aka "the Richmeister," the annoying guy who sat by the office copy machine and bestowed stupid nicknames on everyone who crossed his path. (Musician Sting was in a 1991 "copy guy" skit. His thank-you note to the cast was signed, "Sting. Stingmeister. Der Stingle-hoffer. Sting-a-ling-a-ding-dong.") They soon proved to be the gang that couldn't shoot straight-faced—they constantly cracked one another up on air—and gleefully took things down a notch. Often puerile (and proud of it), they liked their social commentary laced with an ample dose of snark.

Sure, there were highlights: Everyone knew exactly where Farley's pathetic motivational speaker Matt Foley lived ("in a van down by the river!"), and in "The Dark Side with Nat X," Rock's modern angry Black man told his talk show guests to

TRIPPED UP
Above: In 1998, at the height of the Bill Clinton-Monica Lewinsky scandal, Molly Shannon played Lewinsky; Tim Meadows, Clinton adviser Vernon Jordan; and John Goodman, whistleblower Linda Tripp.

BIG NIGHT OUT
Opposite top: Host Jim Carrey (center) joined Chris Kattan (left) and Will Ferrell on the dance floor of the Roxbury to bounce to their favorite song, "What Is Love."

CLUELESS
Opposite right: As oft-exasperated *Celebrity Jeopardy!* host Alex Trebek, Ferrell had to contend with celeb contestants like Robin Williams (Jimmy Fallon), Catherine Zeta-Jones (Lucy Liu) and a hilariously recalcitrant Sean Connery (Darrell Hammond.)

'WHAT IS LOVE?'
—AT THE ROXBURY

HEY, LADIES!
Above: Tim Meadows's Leon Phelps—the Ladies' Man—had a radio call-in show about sex and—always—a tumbler of Courvoisier.

IT'S PAT!
Right: Julia Sweeney's bumbling Pat (with Joe Pesci) was both gender fluid and socially awkward.

I'M OKAY, YOU'RE OKAY
Opposite top: Future U.S. senator Al Franken's "caring nurturer" Stuart Smiley delivered the Daily Affirmation.

LET'S TALK
Opposite bottom: Mike Myers based "Coffee Talk" host Linda Richman on his then-mother-in-law. Her highest praise: "Like buttah."

'I DESERVE GOOD THINGS. I AM ENTITLED TO MY SHARE OF HAPPINESS. I REFUSE TO BEAT MYSELF UP. I AM AN ATTRACTIVE PERSON. I AM FUN TO BE WITH'
—AL FRANKEN AS STUART SMALLEY

"sit yo' ass down" before invariably throwing them out. Sandler's annual performance of his "Chanukah Song" was a clever listing of famous personalities who were Jewish or half Jewish, with Sandler playing guitar.

But wit took a hit, and the ratings did too—up a bit, then way down. In 1991 Hooks, tired of the show's fabled work grind, left to appear on the last two seasons of the sitcom *Designing Women* (though she occasionally returned until 1994, often playing Hillary Clinton). Things were bad enough by late 1991 that Lorne Michaels himself appeared in a skit with host Steve Martin, admitting to Martin that "the show's on automatic pilot." Carvey, whom NBC at one point considered putting in David Letterman's 12:30 slot when Letterman left for CBS, exited in 1993. Hartman said he felt "like an athlete who's watched all his World Series teammates get traded off into other directions.... It was hard to watch them leave because I sort of felt we were all part of the team that saved the show." Finally he left in 1994 and with him the last vestige of grown-up yin to the youthful yang of Sandler and company.

Besieged by TV critics, fans and NBC honchos, Michaels cleaned house. Sandler and Farley were out. Spade survived. (Rock had already left in 1993, Schneider in 1994.) "The *Saturday Night Live* of the mid-1990s must seem like some flavorless leftover that Mom and Dad—those mockable aging baby boomers—refuse to discard from the fridge," *Time* lamented in 1995.

Luckily the F Troop—Ferrell, Fey and Fallon—were waiting in the wings. That year Will Ferrell came on board as East Lake High School Spartan cheerleader Craig. In 1997 Tina Fey was hired as a writer. The next year saw the arrival of a charming kid with an uncanny gift for musical mimicry named Jimmy Fallon. Things were finally looking up.

FEELING OUR PAIN
"We're a political show with a satirical edge, and our basic philosophy is 'Kick 'em when they're down,'" said Phil Hartman (playing President Bill Clinton in 1993). "That's our job."

1948-1998

PHIL HARTMAN

THE BRILLIANT GROWN-UP IN THE ROOM AT *SNL'S* PLAYGROUND

Yet another of the crackerjack Canadians who have graced the show over the years, Ontario-born Hartman spent many years at L.A.'s Groundlings before joining *SNL* in 1986. At 38, he was the oldest member of the cast, "the grandfather of comedy," he noted. Make that wise sage, able to completely inhabit Frank Sinatra or Unfrozen Caveman Lawyer as easily as President Bill Clinton and Chick Hazard, Private Eye. "I benefit from the Mr. Potato Head syndrome," he once said. "Put a wig and a nose and glasses on me, and I disappear." But his consistent brilliance and professionalism were obvious to those around him. "His nickname was the Glue because he held all the sketches together," castmate Kevin Nealon said of Hartman, who was fatally shot by his troubled third wife, Brynn Omdahl, in May 1998. (He was by then starring on *News Radio.*) "If one of us messed up, he covered for us." Fellow *SNL*er Jon Lovitz agreed, calling Hartman "my older brother."

WHAT A NEANDERTHAL!
In 1992 Hartman's Unfrozen Caveman Lawyer successfully argued a case before Ellen Cleghorne, Kevin Nealon, Robert Smigel and Victoria Jackson. Soon after, he ran for U.S. Senate.

LET'S BE FRANK
During a 1991 meeting of "The Sinatra Group," Frank Sinatra (Hartman) called Sinéad O'Connor (Jan Hooks) Uncle Fester and told Billy Idol (Sting), "I got chunks of guys like you in my stool."

'IT'S AN INTENSE EXPERIENCE. YOU START ON TUESDAY MORNING, AND THEN ON FRIDAY YOU'RE DOING DRESS REHEARSALS WITH 10 SKITS. AND LUCKILY THEY HAVE CUE CARDS . . . BUT STILL, THERE IS THE PRESSURE'

—SEVEN-TIME *SNL* HOST CHRISTOPHER WALKEN

BEHIND THE SCENES: CUE CARDS

Cue cards (visible at left during taping of the "The Dumper," with Victoria Jackson and Christopher Walken) are a big part of the show. "It's a live show, and [tele]prompters do break down," explained *SNL* cue-card head Wally Feresten. "Between writers' and actors' changes, which are made right up to—and during!—airtime, they go through 1,000 cards per show. The guest host's cues are always in black ink, the easiest to see."

'BOBBY FISCHER, WHERE IS HE? I DON'T KNOW! I DON'T KNOW! GO ASK YOUR MAMMA AND MAKE SURE YOU LISTEN, 'CAUSE ONE THING IS FOR SURE: BOBBY FISCHER'S MISSIN'

—THE SPARTAN CHEERLEADERS AT A HIGH SCHOOL CHESS MEET

MIND THE GAP
Above: The mallworking Gap Girls—David Spade, Adam Sandler and Chris Farley—often fought with the girls from the food court donut stand.

TOO SEXY
Right: People of all sexual orientations were seduced by Chris Kattan's exotic dancer Mango, based on an actual stripper, Kattan's Russian ex-girlfriend, and his dog.

HIP, HIP, HOORAY!
Opposite: They didn't make the East Lake High School cheerleading squad, but that didn't stop Will Ferrell and Cheri Oteri from showing up on the sidelines anyway.

1964-1997

CHRIS FARLEY

LIKE HIS IDOL, A SUPREMELY GIFTED PHYSICAL COMIC EXITS TOO EARLY

From the beginning, he emulated John Belushi. When Chris Farley arrived from Madison, Wis., where he had always used humor to deflect the torment of growing up overweight, he seemed to occupy the same territory as Belushi, with manic energy and an amazing physicality, displaying an uncanny grace. He had, in fact, played football in high school."He knew how to use his body. He was incredibly funny with it, and, as they say in football, he could play hurt," said Lorne Michaels. Farley must have been hurt a lot. Crashing through a coffee table, as he famously did as motivational speaker Matt Foley, or sweating through a grueling Chippendales audition against a trained dancer, host Patrick Swayze (opposite, left), takes its physical and emotional toll. "Fatty falls down," he said too modestly of his appeal. Unfortunately, like Belushi, Farley suffered from addiction to drugs and alcohol. He died of an overdose of cocaine and opiates, in 1997, at just 33.

'IN A VAN DOWN BY THE RIVER'
Chris Farley's motivational speaker Matt Foley took on boxer George Foreman in 1994 (top). Interviewing Paul McCartney on "The Chris Farley Show," he asked, "Remember *Beatlemania*, when four guys dressed like you and played Beatles' songs?"

BAD SANTA
Motivational Santa's message to the mall kids: "You hang [a stocking] up, and the next morning you find it filled to the brim with jack squat!"

'CHRIS AND I GOT TO BE REALLY CLOSE. IT BROKE MY HEART WHEN HE DIED. I ACTUALLY SAW HIM THE NIGHT BEFORE, AND I TRIED TO TALK TO HIM, BUT HE WAS IN THAT KIND OF MOMENT, GONE, NOT HERE'
—PATRICK SWAYZE, 2005

THE BEST MUSICAL PERFORMANCES
>SNL< THE '90s

NO WAY! WAY!
Above: Aerosmith first showed up in his breakfast nook before Wayne of "Wayne's World" invited band members Brad Whitford, Steven Tyler, Joe Perry, Joey Kramer (hidden) and Tom Hamilton downstairs to play his theme song.

PRIME TIME
Left: Whitney Houston was as the height of her vocal splendor during her 1991 guest spot, singing her hits "I'm Your Baby Tonight" and "All The Man That I Need."

GRUNGE KINGS
Opposite top: Nirvana dropped by in 1993 to perform "Heart-Shaped Box." Right: Led by lead singer Eddie Vedder, fellow Seattleites Pearl Jam performed "Alive" in 1992.

'PUT ON A YARMULKE, HERE COMES CHANUKAH'

Above: New Hampshire's own *SNL* cast member Adam Sandler debuted his "Chanukah Song" in December 1994, dedicated to all the Jewish kids who on Christmas "only had the song 'Dreidel, Dreidel, Dreidel.'" Sample lyric: "You don't need 'Deck the Halls' or 'Jingle Bell Rock,' 'cause you can spin a dreidel with Captain Kirk and Mr. Spock (both Jewish!)."

BEY AND THE BOYS
Beyoncé thought the dancers for a 2008 skit on the filming of her "Single Ladies (Put a Ring on It)" video "would be strong, beautiful women," she said. Instead she got (from right) Justin Timberlake, Bobby Moynihan and Andy Samberg.

SATURDAY NIGHT LIVE
The BEST of the '00s

S*ATURDAY NIGHT LIVE* HIT THE NEW MILLENNIUM RUNNING. Strong political parodies featured Will Ferrell's chronically confused George W. Bush and Darrell Hammond's ever-sighing, sanctimonious Al Gore—and coanchors Tina Fey and Jimmy Fallon brought a refreshingly sly spin to "Weekend Update." But 2001's premiere came just 18 days after the 9/11 attacks. In the poignant opener, Lorne Michaels asked then-mayor of New York City Rudolph Giuliani, surrounded by members of the New York City police and fire departments, "Can we be funny?" The mayor deadpanned, "Why start now?" then turned to the audience and delivered the show's famous opening line.

In the decade to come, *SNL* showcased sparkling writing and a strong cast ensemble. Kenan Thompson headlined the talk show "What Up with That?," whose host Diondre Cole burst into song and continually drowned out guests (who included the real former Vice President Al Gore). Will Forte was the hapless MacGruber—a clever play on *MacGyver,* the famed special-operations agent from '80s TV who ingeniously used what was at hand to save the day. MacGruber tried to make do with rubber bands and gum wrappers—and the ticking time bomb went off at the end of every sketch.

Out went the explosive, often troubled comics of previous decades, and in came the "trained assassins," as Michaels called his posse of remarkable female comedians. Fey, the show's first woman head writer, occasionally popped out from behind the "Weekend Update" desk to prove she was just as adept as a sketch comedian. Amy Poehler (who would join Fey as a news coanchor in 2004) was a burst

'MORE COWBELL'
—CHRISTOPHER WALKEN AS FAMED MUSIC PRODUCER BRUCE DICKINSON

CLASSIC ROCK
Left: In one of *SNL*'s most famous skits, Will Ferrell (center) played fictional Blue Oyster Cult member Gene Frenkle, providing over-the-top handheld percussion for the band's real-life 1976 hit "(Don't Fear)The Reaper" under the direction of "producer" Christopher Walken.

BEHIND THE SCENES: RUNNING LINES

Below: Host Jennifer Lopez and Chris Kattan confer before they hit the stage as competing divas in 2001's "J.Lo vs. Mango," in which they trashed their shared dressing room and wrestled onstage.

NEW GIRL AT THE BADA BING
In 2007 Molly Shannon returned as host and performed as mature hoofer Sally O'Malley, who auditioned for a stripper job at the *Sopranos'* Bada Bing club. "The caboose may be a little loose," O'Malley said, but "I like to kick, stretch and KICK! I'm 50!"

of energy, whether as hyperactive preteen Kaitlin or exuberant morning talk show host Kelly Ripa. Her gum-chomping Betty joined Maya Rudolph's Jodi as blunt-talking housewives in the women's talk show "Bronx Beat," when Rudolph wasn't imitating a who's who of celebs like Beyoncé and diva designer Donatella Versace. Rachel Dratch was riotous as eternal glass-half-empty gal Debbie Downer and provided a wicked Massachusetts accent for Boston-area teen Denise, in love with Fallon's Sully. All four of them came together for one of the skits that have since entered the lexicon: "Mom Jeans." Frolicking through suburbia with way-high waists and baggy bottoms, wearers of Mom Jeans let the world know "I'm not a woman anymore. I'm a mom!" And this was even before Kristen Wiig showed up in 2005 in the person of the nosy Target Lady, the violently disruptive schoolgirl Gilly, the vapid teenage A-Hole and a list of impressions long enough to circle 30 Rock.

That same year "Digital Shorts" transformed *SNL* yet again, catching fire with the nerd rap "Lazy Sunday," in which wannabe tough guys Chris Parnell and Andy Samberg get cupcakes from Magnolia Bakery (of *Sex and the City* fame) and go see *The Chronicles of Narnia.* Ushering the show into the digital age, "Digital Shorts" also brought in younger fans, who "liked" the follow-ups, including "I'm on a Boat" and the blockbuster "D--- in a Box."

But nothing topped Election 2008 and Tina Fey's uncanny impersonation of Alaska governor Sarah Palin. Also featuring Poehler's Hillary Clinton, *SNL's* campaign spoofs routinely got nearly as much press as the actual candidates. The year's indelible meta-moment came on Oct. 18, when the real and fake Sarah Palins appeared in the same sketch (passing each other at a press conference), drawing the show's biggest audience in 14 years. "I just thought, 'Well, that's what they'll show when I die,'" said Fey, who originally didn't want to do it. She is probably right.

BEHIND THE SCENES: OTHER SIDE OF THE CAMERA

Above: After appearing in a 2005 Hurricane Katrina benefit concert at which Kanye West said President George W. Bush "doesn't care about Black people," the rapper and Mike Myers reunited when West was the musical guest on *SNL* four weeks later, performing "Gold Digger." Below: Kenan Thompson (here, in 2015) debuted Diondre Cole, the never-stop-singing host of "What Up with That," in season 35 in 2009.

LIGHTEN UP!
Above: The Matusick clan—from left, Jimmy Fallon, Rachel Dratch, Amy Poehler, Fred Armisen, host Lindsay Lohan and Horatio Sanz—was trying to enjoy a trip to Disney World, but perpetual pessimist Debbie Downer (Dratch, left) was just that in 2004.

ANIMAL MAGNETISM
Opposite top: On "Brian Fellow's Safari Planet" Tracy Morgan's tetchy amateur zoologist had "a sixth-grade education and an abiding love for all God's creatures."

SHE'S A LOT
Opposite bottom: Kristen Wiig's Penelope (left) was the hyper-competitive neighbor of Shannon, Poehler and Thompson at a 2007 tenants meeting.

'I'M BRIAN FELLOW'
—"BRIAN FELLOW'S SAFARI PLANET" HOST

BEHIND THE SCENES: MAKEUP

In the makeup chair, Armisen (left) was made into President Barack Obama while nearby Darrell Hammond became Senator John McCain before a 2008 debate.

GORE VS. BUSH

In the first 2000 presidential debate, Al Gore (Hammond, left) introduced his "lock box" plan for Medicare. George W. Bush (Ferrell) warned him: "Don't mess with Texas."

HILLARY CLINTON: 'I BELIEVE THAT DIPLOMACY SHOULD BE THE CORNERSTONE OF ANY FOREIGN POLICY.' SARAH PALIN: 'AND I CAN SEE RUSSIA FROM MY HOUSE'
—FEY (LEFT, AS PALIN) AND POEHLER (AS CLINTON) IN 2008

JUSTIN TIMBERLAKE
>SNL<
THE '00s
FAVORITE GUEST STAR

SWEET CHARITY
Above: In 2006 Will Forte (left), as a Santa collecting donations for the Salvation Army, had to compete with Justin Timberlake's hip-hop Cup O' Soup mascot soliciting funds for a homeless shelter.

BULLSEYE
Left: In 2009 Peg (Timberlake) told Wiig's Target Lady what was on her shopping list: "Potato sticks and car oil. I got a date tonight." Oh, and satin handcuffs.

BRING IN THE BACKUP
Bottom left: Host Paul Rudd (right) faux-directed Beyoncé's 2008 "Single Ladies" video with Timberlake (far left). "Why are his legs more beautiful than any woman's?" the singer asked.

UNCANNY LIKENESS
Opposite: In 2003 Timberlake popped in as Bee Gee Robin Gibb to duet with brother Barry (Fallon) on "The Barry Gibb Show."

'I GAVE SOME SUGGESTIONS ON HOW TO DO ME BETTER. BECAUSE I TOLD HER I DON'T DRINK. TAKE OFF THAT JEWELRY, BECAUSE [IT'S] TOO FAKE; I ONLY WEAR REAL'
—THE REAL DONATELLA VERSACE

DESIGNING WOMAN
Maya Rudolph played Italian fashion designer Donatella Versace with ever-present cigarette, furious temper and usually champagne. In 2003 supermodel Naomi Campbell (host Halle Berry, right) crashed Versace's Halloween party.

THE BEST MUSICAL PERFORMANCES
>SNL<
THE '00s

BANDSTAND
Above: In 2005 former No Doubt singer Gwen Stefani brought a marching band with her to perform her solo hit "Hollaback Girl."

HOT IN HERE
Left: Montreal-based indie darlings Arcade Fire made the first of five appearances in 2007.

BEST FAIL
Below left: For Ashlee Simpson, Oct. 23, 2004, will live in infamy. She was caught lip-syncing when a track of her song *Pieces of Me* played twice.

COOL KID
Far left: In 2006 iconoclastic superstar Beck performed "Nausea" and "Clap Hands."

TOP OF THE POP
In October 2008 *SNL* welcomed British sensation Adele, singing her lost-love hit "Chasing Pavements."

SATURDAY NIGHT LIVE

The BEST of the '10s

SHE'S BACK!
As host in 2013, Kristen Wiig returned to *SNL* and reprised her deranged Dooneese (far right) in an inspired parody of *The Sound of Music* (with, clockwise from left, Kate McKinnon, Beck Bennett, Cecily Strong, Bobby Moynihan, Noël Wells and Nasim Pedrad).

FREEZE FRAME
An NBC promo for Wiig's second return as host in 2016 featured the cast doing the then-popular mannequin challenge—standing stock still in a staged tableau.

IN THE FIRST FOUR YEARS OF THE DECADE, *Saturday Night Live* vacillated between mediocrity and brilliance. That of, course, is nothing new. The show has faced the premature Saturday Night Dead criticisms since the early 1980s. But this era has seen a series of unusually difficult transitions. Kristen Wiig, one of the show's all-time greats, left, along with such other major talents as Fred Armisen, Andy Samberg, Bill Hader and Jason Sudeikis (all of whom have gone on to success on screens both big and small).

Slowly but surely, however, a new team was being built. Vanessa Bayer was promoted to repertory player in 2012, the same year that saw the arrival of Kate McKinnon, Cecily Strong and Aidy Bryant. For the 2013-14 season, in what former head writer Tina Fey called a "rebuilding year," six new cast members were added, including Beck Bennett and Kyle Mooney. Under head writer Colin Jost, it was turbulent (and Bennett and Mooney were the only two of those six to return). Early in the season "Weekend Update" host Seth Meyers announced he would be leaving at the end to take over Jimmy Fallon's spot on *Late Night* (Jost was tagged to replace him). The show came under criticism for not having a black female cast member, so producer Lorne Michaels announced auditions. The winner: former Upright Citizens Brigade performer Sasheer Zamata. Fall 2014 brought more arrivals that further diversified *SNL's* stage roster: Writer Leslie Jones was promoted to cast player, and former writer Michael Che returned from *The Daily Show*

FRIGHTENING
Top: Kenan Thompson operated 2016's "Haunted Elevator," where Bennett and McKinnon met Halloween star David S. Pumpkins (Tom Hanks).

DELICIOUS DISH
Above: Betty White guested on Ana Gasteyer's (left) and Molly Shannon's naughty NPR food show in 2010.

LADIES' MEN
Left: On "ESPN Classic," Pete Twinkle (Jason Sudeikis, left) and Greg Stink (Will Forte) covered women's sports as best they could.

'WHEN I FIRST STARTED AT *SNL*, I COULDN'T BELIEVE MY FACE WAS ON THE SHOW. [NOW] I'M GOING TO TRY TO MAKE THAT RECORD AS LONG AS POSSIBLE'
—KENAN THOMPSON, THE SHOW'S LONGEST-RUNNING CAST MEMBER

to cohost "Weekend Update." Also new and noteworthy: Off-kilter stand-up comedian Pete Davidson, the first *SNL*er to be born in the '90s, joined the cast after the departure in 2014 of Iranian-born Nasim Pedrad, who won fame for her annoying nasal impression of reality superstar Kim Kardashian. The revolving casting door has slowed down since mid-decade, but when the show hired new talent, as it did in 2017 for black stand-up comedian Chris Redd and in 2019 for Bowen Yang—the third openly gay male and first Chinese-American cast member—*SNL* more accurately reflected the America on the other side of the screen.

And that America has certainly given *SNL* plenty of material to work with during the past decade. With two of the most contentious elections in U.S. history taking place in 2016 and 2020, the show has brought out the big guns to take on the headlines: Tina Fey's preternaturally perfect Sarah Palin; Amy Poehler's uncanny Hillary Clinton; Alec Baldwin as a peerless Donald Trump (lately going against a rotating cast of Joe Bidens); and superstar McKinnon, as a homespun and straight-talking Elizabeth Warren. *SNL*'s weekly take on what can seem like a surreal political circus often makes more headlines—and more sense—than the candidates themselves. And it's certainly more entertaining. "In our world it doesn't sort of matter which side you're on," Lorne Michaels once said. "As long as it's funny."

DAILY DOUBLE
Above: "This may be the blackest *Black Jeopardy!* ever," declared host Kenan Thompson when *Black Panther* star Chadwick Boseman (far right) appeared with Leslie Jones and Chris Redd in 2018.

READY OR NOT
Top left: Playing a doctor, 2018 host Jessica Chastain's temperature rose for her patient, Pete Davidson's total bro Chad.

NO. 1 LOBSTER
Opposite: In a 2018 musical parody of *Les Mis,* valiant waiter John Mulaney saved Thompson's Diner Lobster from death.

'LET'S RIDE'
Bottom left: Bowen Yang's eerily intense Flint ("like the water") auditioned to be a SoulCycle instructor in 2019.

SELLING IT
In 2014 none-too-bright spokesmodels Vanessa Bayer (center) and Strong had help from Seth Rogen (left) and host James Franco on a TV commercial promoting "yaw-kets" (yachts).

'WE AREN'T PORN STARS ANYMORE'
—THE FORMER PORN STARS

ANCHOR LUST
During her many visits to "WU," Leslie Jones made no bones about her crush on host Jost, calling him "you delectable Caucasian" and other terms of endearment.

WEEKENDUPDATEWEEKENDUPDATE

RED-BLOODED
Left: Smokery Farms sisters Vaneta and Wylene Starkie (McKinnon, left, and Aidy Bryant) pressed their wares on "Weekend Update" hosts Colin Jost and Michael Che in 2019.

OUT THERE
Right: From 2010 to 2013, Bill Hader's urban correspondent Stefon (with host Seth Myers) guided viewers to nightclubs featuring screaming babies in Mozart wigs. He broke character nearly every time.

NAILED IT
Below: Melissa Villaseñor's Lady Gaga-loving entertainment commentator delivered a spot-on rendition of "Shallow"before the Oscars in 2019.

'I WASN'T AT THE JIM CARREY AUDITION, BUT SOMEBODY WHO WAS THERE SAID, "I DON'T THINK LORNE WOULD LIKE IT"...NO ONE GETS IT ALL RIGHT'

—LORNE MICHAELS ON CARREY, WHO DIDN'T MAKE THE CAST

DANCE OFF
Both dressed as the little girl in Sia's "Chandelier" video, coworkers Jim Carrey and McKinnon spilled offstage during a hyperkinetic duel for the prize at the office costume party in 2014.

'I HAVE 10 KIDS NOW, 11 IF YOU COUNT KEVIN HART . . . IF YOU HAD TOLD ME 30 YEARS AGO THAT I WOULD BE THIS BORING, STAY-AT-HOME HOUSEDAD AND BILL COSBY WOULD BE IN JAIL, EVEN I WOULD HAVE TOOK THAT BET'

—**EDDIE MURPHY**

KINGS OF COMEDY

Thirty-five years after he left *SNL* in 1984, Eddie Murphy returned as host of the 2019 holiday show and busted out some of the old favorites. Clockwise from above: During his monologue he was joined onstage by (left to right) Tracy Morgan, Dave Chappelle and Chris Rock; he reminded "Weekend Update" host Che, "How the hell are people not going to know who I am? I'm Gumby, damn it!"; when he played a contestant on Holiday Baking Championship, his Speedy the Hedgehog cake turned out all brown; in "Mr. Robinson's Neighborhood," he bemoaned gentrification, saying, "It's like a magic trick. White people pay a lot of money, and then poof! All the black people are gone."

FINAL ACT
Above: Prince's nearly nine-minute 2014 performance was the last of the legend's four *SNL* sets and one of the most memorable in TV history.

WILDLY HARRY
Right: Former One Direction member Harry Styles not only sang during a 2017 visit, he played Mick Jagger in "Celebrity Family Feud."

BLESSED
Opposite top: In 2018 rapper Cardi B chose a skintight Christian Siriano dress to reveal her baby bump after weeks of pregnancy rumors.

HAIR TOSS
Opposite bottom: On the 2019 holiday show, pop phenomenon Lizzo delivered a festive version of her hit "Good as Hell."

'CONGRATULATIONS TO MY GIRL @IAMCARDIB, NEW BABY ON THE WAY! YOU LOOKED STUNNING TONIGHT IN CUSTOM SIRIANO ON @NBCSNL IT WAS AN HONOR. #CARDIB'

—DESIGNER CHRISTIAN SIRIANO

THE POLITICIANS
>SNL<
THE '10s
THE IMPERSONATORS

GOING VIRAL
Above: Host John Mulaney (left) was Joe Biden, Bennett was Vice President Mike Pence, and McKinnon played Elizabeth Warren during a 2020 spoof of a press conference about coronavirus.

ON A ROLL
Opposite: As *SNL's* resident President, Alec Baldwin promised at a 2017 Trump rally that "we're going to start saying Merry Christmas again, and you cannot disrespect our lord and savior, Santa Claus."

CAPITAL RESPONSE
"Spicey's back!" yelled Melissa McCarthy before her then-White House press secretary Sean Spicer went ballistic during a 2017 press briefing.

'THE FIRST SEASON, FUN, FUN, FUN. [NOW] I ALWAYS SAY TO MYSELF, "PEOPLE ARE SICK OF THIS"... BUT THEN I GO OUT AT NIGHT, AND 50 PEOPLE SAY, "KEEP GOING." THEY NEED THIS TO MANAGE THEIR PAIN'

—ALEC BALDWIN ON PLAYING TRUMP

IT'S DEBATABLE
Real news or fake? *SNL*'s Sen. Bernie Sanders (Larry David, left), Sen. Kamala Harris (Maya Rudolph) and Tom Steyer (Will Ferrell) faced off during the Democratic primaries in 2019.

CREDITS

FRONT COVER
(Clockwise from top right) Will Heath/NBCU Photo Bank/NBCUniversal/Getty Images; NBC/NBCU Photo Bank/Getty Images; Alan Singer/NBCU Photo Bank/NBCUniversal/Getty Images; Chris Haston/NBCU Photo Bank/NBCUniversal/Getty Images; NBC/Everett Collection; NBC/NBCU Photo Bank/Getty Images; Dana Edelson/NBC/NBCU Photo Bank Universal/Getty Images; NBC/NBCU Photo Bank/Getty Images; NBC/Everett Collection; Will Heath/NBCU Photo Bank/NBCUniversal/Getty Images

TITLE PAGE
1 Copyright Edie Baskin, 1977

TABLE OF CONTENTS
2-3 T'heo Wargo/NBCU Photo Bank/NBCUniversal/Getty Images

FOREWORD
4-5 Will Heath/NBCU Photo Bank/NBCUniversal/Getty Images; **6** NBC/NBCU Photo Bank/Getty Images; NBC; **7** NBC/NBCU Photo Bank/Getty Images; **8-9** Ralph Bavaro/NBCU Photo Bank/NBCUniversal/Getty Images

1970s
10-11 Ken Regan/Camera 5; **12-13** NBC/NBCU Photo Bank/Getty Images(2); **14-15** (from top) NBC/NBCU Photo Bank/Getty Images(2); Alan Singer/NBCU Photo Bank/NBCUniversal/Getty Images; **16** (from top) NBC/NBCU Photo Bank/Getty Images; Alan Singer/NBCU Photo Bank/NBCUniversal/Getty Images; **17** Everett Collection; **18** Alan Singer/NBCU Photo Bank/NBCUniversal/Getty Images; **19** (from top) NBC/NBCU Photo Bank/Getty Images; NBC/Photofest(2); **20** (from top) Owen Franken/Corbis/Getty Images; NBC; **21** (from top) NBC/NBCU Photo Bank/Getty Images; NBC/Everett; **22** (from top) Al Levine/NBCU Photo Bank/NBCUniversal/Getty Images; NBC/NBCU Photo Bank/Getty Images(2); **23** Owen Franken/Corbis/Getty Images; **24** NBC/NBCU Photo Bank/Getty Images; **25** NBC/NBCU Photo Bank/Getty Images(3); **26** NBC/NBCU Photo Bank/Getty Images; **27** Fred Bronson/NBCU Photo Bank/NBCUniversal/Getty Images

1980s
28-29 Alan Singer/NBCU Photo Bank/NBCUniversal/Getty Images; **30-31** NBC/NBCU Photo Bank/Getty Images(2); **32-33** (clockwise from top left) Fred Hermansky/NBC/NBCU Photo Bank/Getty Images; Raymond Bonar/NBCU Photo Bank/NBCUniversal/Getty Images; NBC/NBCU Photo Bank/Getty Images; **34-35** Al Levine/NBCU Photo Bank/NBCUniversal/Getty Images(2); **35** (top) NBC/NBCU Photo Bank/Getty Images; **36** NBC/NBCU Photo Bank/Getty Images; **37** (from top) Alan Singer/NBCU Photo Bank/NBCUniversal/Getty Images; NBC; Raymond Bonar/NBCU Photo Bank/NBCUniversal/Getty Images; **38** (from top) Al Levine/NBCU Photo Bank/NBCUniversal/Getty Images; NBC/Everett; **39** Alan Singer/NBCU Photo Bank/NBCUniversal/Getty Images; **40** Raymond Bonar/NBCU Photo Bank/NBCUniversal/Getty Images; **41** (from top) RM Lewis Jr./NBCU Photo Bank/NBCUniversal/Getty Images; NBC/Photofest; NBC/NBCU Photo Bank/Getty Images; **42** Alan Singer/NBCU Photo Bank/NBCUniversal/Getty Images(3); **43** Al Levine/NBCU Photo Bank/NBCUniversal/Getty Images

1990s
44-45 NBC/NBCU Photo Bank/Getty Images; **46** NBC/ Everett Collection; **47** (from top) Al Levine/NBCU Photo Bank/NBCUniversal /Getty Images; Dana Edelson/NBC/NBCU Photo Bank Universal/Getty Images; **48** (from top) Mary Ellen Matthews/NBCU Photo Bank/Getty Images; NBC/NBCU Photo Bank/Getty Images; **49** (from top) Dana Edelson/NBCU Photo Bank/NBCUniversal /Getty Images; Norman Ng/NBCU Photo Bank/NBCUniversal/Getty Images; **50** Gerry Goodstein/NBCU Photo Bank/NBCUniversal/Getty Images; **51** (from top) Al Levine/NBCU Photo Bank/NBCUniversal/Getty Images; Alan Singer/NBCU Photo Bank/NBCUniversal/Getty Images; **52-53** Alan Singer/NBCU Photo Bank/NBCUniversal/Getty Images; **54** Al Levine/NBCU Photo Bank/NBCUniversal/Getty Images; **55** (from top) Dana Edelson/NBCU Photo Bank/NBCUniversal/Getty Images; Gerry Goodstein/NBCU Photo Bank/NBCUniversal/Getty Images; **56** (from top) Al Levine/NBCU Photo Bank/NBCUniversal/Getty Images(2); Gene Page/NBCU Photo Bank/NBCUniversal/Getty Images; **57** Al Levine/NBCU Photo Bank/NBCUniversal/Getty Images; **58** Raymond Bonar/NBCU Photo Bank/NBCUniversal/Getty Images(2); **59** (clockwise from top) Al Levine/NBCU Photo Bank/NBCUniversal/Getty Images; Alan Singer/NBCU Photo Bank/NBCUniversal/Getty Images; Gerry Goodstein/NBCU Photo Bank/NBCUniversal/Getty Images

2000s
60-61 Alan Singer/NBCU Photo Bank/NBCUniversal/Getty Images; **62-63** Mary Ellen Matthews/NBCU Photo Bank/Getty Images(2); **64-65** (from top) Dana Edelson/NBCU Photo Bank/NBCUniversal/Getty Images(2); Theo Wargo/NBCU Photo Bank/NBCUniversal/Getty Images; **66-67** Dana Edelson/NBCU Photo Bank/NBCUniversal/Getty Images(4); **68** (from top) Charles Ommanney/Getty Images; Dana Edelson/NBC/NBCU Photo Bank/

Universal/Getty Images; **69** Dana Edelson/NBC/NBCU Photo Bank/Universal/Getty Images; **70-71** Dana Edelson/NBCU Photo Bank/NBCUniversal/Getty Images(4); **72-73** Mary Ellen Matthews/NBCU Photo Bank/Getty Images; **74-77** Dana Edelson/NBCU Photo Bank/NBCUniversal/Getty Images(5)

2010s
76-77 Dana Edelson/NBCU Photo Bank/NBCUniversal/Getty Images; **78** Rosalind O'Connor/NBCU Photo Bank/NBCUniversal/Getty Images; **79** (from top) Will Heath/NBCU Photo Bank/NBCUniversal/Getty Images; Dana Edelson/NBC/NBCU Photo Bank Universal/Getty Images(2); **80** Will Heath/NBCU Photo Bank/NBCUniversal/Getty Images(2); **81** (from top) Kailey Fellows/NBCU Photo Bank/NBCUniversal/Getty Images; Will Heath/NBCU Photo Bank/NBCUniversal/Getty Images; **82-83** Dana Edelson/NBCU Photo Bank/NBCUniversal/Getty Images; **84** (from top) Will Heath/NBCU Photo Bank/NBCUniversal/Getty Images; Dana Edelson/NBC/NBCU Photo Bank Universal/Getty Images; **85** (from top) Dana Edelson/NBC/NBCU Photo Bank Universal/Getty Images(2); Will Heath/NBCU Photo Bank/NBCUniversal/Getty Images; **86-87** Dana Edelson/NBCU Photo Bank/NBCUniversal /Getty Images; **88-94** All Photos by Will Heath/NBCU Photo Bank/NBCUniversal/Getty Images

END
96 Dana Edelson/NBC/NBCU Photo Bank Universal/Getty Images

BACK COVER
(Clockwise from top left) Ken Regan/Camera 5; Andrew Eccles/NBCU Photo Bank/NBCUniversal/Getty Images; Dana Edelson/NBC/NBCU Photo Bank Universal/Getty Images; NBC/ Everett Collection; Mary Ellen Matthews/NBCU Photo Bank/Getty Images; NBC/NBCU Photo Bank/Getty Images; NBC/Photofest; Alan Singer/NBCU Photo Bank/NBCUniversal/Getty Images; NBC/NBCU Photo Bank/Getty Images; Dana Edelson/NBC/NBCU Photo Bank Universal/Getty Images

GOOD NIGHT

In the tradition established from the first broadcasts in the 1970s, the *Saturday Night Live* 40th-anniversary special ended on Feb. 15, 2015, with cast members, celebrity hosts and musical guests gathered onstage to bid the studio and TV audience good night. Seen here: Lorne Michaels (center) with Dan Aykroyd, Jim Belushi, Jim Carrey, Miley Cyrus, Jimmy Fallon, Tina Fey, James Franco, Leslie Jones, Jon Lovitz, Steve Martin, Paul McCartney, Norm Macdonald, Tim Meadows, Garrett Morris, Chris Rock, Andy Samberg, Justin Timberlake and many others.

Printed in Great Britain
by Amazon

60851862R00056